UNDERSTANDING IMMIGRATION

Life as an Immigrant

Iris Teichmann

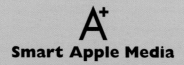

A⁺
Smart Apple Media

First published in 2005 by Franklin Watts
96 Leonard Street, London EC2A 4XD

Franklin Watts Australia
Level 17/207 Kent Street
Sydney NSW 2000

Series editor: Rachel Cooke
Series design: Simon Borrough
Picture research: Diana Morris

Published in the United States by Smart Apple Media
2140 Howard Drive West, North Mankato, Minnesota 56003

Library of Congress Cataloging-in-Publication Data

Teichmann, Iris.
Life as an immigrant / by Iris Teichmann.
p. cm. — (Understanding immigration)
Includes index.
ISBN-13 : 978-1-58340-968-8
1. Emigration and immigration—Juvenile literature. 2. Immigrants—Juvenile literature. I. Title.

JV6035.T45 2006
305.9'06912—dc22   2005051737

9 8 7 6 5 4 3 2 1

Acknowledgements: The author and publishers would like to thank all those people who were interviewed for this book. In addition, we would also like to acknowledge the following sources: Theodore's story, p. 10, David Kuhns, www.geocities.com/Athens/Forum/4074starkege.htm. Bernardus's story, p.11, Charmaine Nolte and Pier21. Yu Hui's story, p.12, the *Guardian*, 12.18.2004. Bernabe's story, p.14, Bernabe Garay, "A Migrant Harvester's Letters Home," in *The Fight in the Fields: Cesar Chavez and the Farmworkers Movement*, Harcourt. Yuriy's story, p.15, Jesuit Refugee Service. Abed's story. p.16, British Refugee Council. Aduei's story, p. 17, International Organization for Migration, *World Migration*, 2003. An entrepreneur's story, p.19, Trine Lund Thomsen, AMID, "Immigrant Entrepreneurship: A Struggle for Social Recognition — a working paper." Abdul's story, p.20, British Refugee Council. Edris's story, p. 22, British Refugee Council. Maziah's story, p.23, M. Enriquez-Olmos, *Personal Narratives: Educational Concerns of Foreign and Immigrant Parents*, University of Denver. A family's story, p.24, Elizabeth C. Watson, *Home Work in the Tenements*, Survey 25 (February 4, 1911), 772-781. Yanira's story, p.27, Emily Brady, *The Petaluma Argus Courier*. Tina's story, p.28, Oracle Education Foundation/ThinkQuest at http://library.thinkquest.org (History/Government, United States, The Great Melting Pot, Immigration). Thilepan's story, p. 29, BBC News, Talking Point, 8/6/2001. Ayman's story, p.30, Quaker Council for European Affairs Network. Warsan's story, p.31, "Listen to the Refugee Story: How UK Foreign Investment Creates Refugees and Asylum Seekers," Ilisu Dam Campaign Refugees Project, The Corner House and Peace in Kurdistan, 2003. Madrigal's story, p.34, Barry Yeoman, "Silence in the Fields," *Mother Jones Magazine*, January/February 2001 issue. Meng Dong's story, p.36, David Jonathan Epstein, *Downtown Express*, Volume 16, Issue 38, February 20–26, 2004. Kuei and Yai's story, p.38, Sanctuary Refugee Foundation, New South Wales, Australia. Nazar's story, p.39, British Refugee Council. Mark's story, p.41, www.sentimentalrefugee.com

Photographic credits:
Ace Stock Ltd/Alamy: p.35. Sabah Arar/Rex Features: p.39tl. Bangladesh Center, Houston: p.20. © Zafir Behlic: p.33. Trygve Bølstad/Panos: p.37. © British Refugee Council: p.31. Corbis: p.8. H. Davies/Exile Images: pp.9, 16, 28, 29, 39br, 40. Dave Gately/Rex Features: p.34. © Rose Kaye: p.32. Ute Klaphake/Photofusion: front cover b, pp.2, 3, 4, 45, 46, 47. Peter Lomas/Rex Features: p.12. Minnesota Historical Society/Corbis: p.10. © Namarata Nayar: p.26b. © Charmaine Nolte: p.11tr. Photofusion/Alamy: pp.26c, 27. Picturepoint/Topham: p.23. Rex Features: p.11bl. Jacob August Riis/Bettmann/Corbis: p.24. Lorena Ross/Panos: p.15. © Sanctuary Refugee Foundation, New South Wales, Australia: p.38. Phil Schermeister/Corbis: p.41. Harmut Schwarzbach/Still Pictures: p.19. Qilai Shen/Panos: p.36. Sipa Press/Rex Features: front cover t, pp.13, 14, 30. Lesley Smith/Rex Features: p.25. Paula Solloway/Photofusion: p.17. Ray Tang/Rex Features: p.18. J. L.Tordai/Panos: p.21. Jaime Turner/Rex Features: p.22.

Contents

Who are immigrants?   8

Working in a new country   10

Barriers to work   16

Immigrant communities   20

Settling in   26

Making a mark   34

Thinking of the future   38

Glossary   42

Web connections   43

Index   44

Who are immigrants?

A street vendor sells fresh oysters to Italian immigrants in Little Italy, New York, in the late 19th century.

Immigrants are people who have settled in another country. They stop being immigrants if they become nationals of the country they have settled in. Migrants are people who work abroad for a short period of time only, but they can become immigrants if they decide to stay. Millions of people around the world are immigrants. They have left their homes to live in another country to work, to build new lives or careers, or simply to experience life abroad.

Opportunities

How would you feel about going to live in another country? Moving abroad takes courage and initiative. Immigrants are often resourceful people who work hard to build a new life even though they may not always be able to fulfill their dream of pursuing a particular career or building an ideal future for their children. Immigrants have shaped societies all over the world by bringing new skills, customs, and ideas, and paying taxes to their new country. The United States and Australia are two nations that have been shaped by their immigrant populations.

Challenges

Building a new life abroad can be difficult. Immigrants have to deal with unfamiliar laws and customs. They have to get used to a new language and to new government systems, such as education and healthcare. Many immigrants have problems finding a job if they don't speak the language of their new country well or if they cannot use the skills they already have. Life can be particularly hard if there is local prejudice or hostility toward immigrant communities.

AS A MATTER OF FACT

The term "immigrant" covers legal and illegal immigration. Immigrants therefore include the following groups of people: those who have traveled legally and are allowed to stay in their new country, those who may have traveled to a country illegally but have then achieved legal status, and those who have arrived illegally and continue to stay in the country illegally.

Fitting in

Much of the political discussion on immigration today is about how much immigrants should adapt to their new home. Most developed countries prefer immigrants to identify more fully with local customs and culture. Many immigrants, especially the younger generation, are happy to do this, but others prefer to keep to their own communities. Immigrants, particularly refugees, often hope to return home at some point in the future.

A refugee couple receives some language guidance to help them start to build a new life in a new country.

9

Working in a new country

The first priority for any migrant or immigrant when arriving in a new country is to find work. This is because no matter what a person's motive is for moving abroad, work provides an income, stability, and the possibility of building a future for oneself and one's family. Even for people who have left their country because of war or persecution, once they are safe in another country, the immediate desire is to find work that will help them become independent and build a future.

A helping hand

Many immigrants have gone through a lot of financial sacrifices to move abroad, which makes finding a job all the more important. While some may already have a job waiting for them when they arrive, the majority do not, and it can take some time to find out where to go and who to talk to in order to find work. Many seek help and advice from family members or friends who have already settled in the country or from community contacts.

THEODORE'S STORY: GETTING BY IN AMERICA

Theodore Kestner left Germany for a new life in Wisconsin in the late 1800s. He had regular contact with his other relatives who had also immigrated to America, such as Bertha Starke, to whom he wrote asking for help:

"As I have heard, it is going well for you. It's going sadly for us. This year we couldn't plant and harvest any feed for the cattle, and can't buy any more now. If we [hadn't] bought a horse and granary tools, we would have had to walk away from [the farm]. We have a lot of land, but [to work] by hand is impossible. I ask please once again, from my heart, for $5, if possible, really soon."

A small, 19th-century farm in the U.S.'s newly settled Midwest.

Going it alone

Immigrants are not entitled to financial help from the government when they arrive—such help may only come after they have lived and worked in the country for a while. If they arrive on their own, they have no support from other people and will often accept the first job they can find, even if it is not what they wanted to do or if it is hard or badly paid. A lot of the jobs offered are on a temporary or, in some cases, daily basis.

A migrant worker waits hopefully to be hired for a day's laboring on a building site.

BERNARDUS'S STORY: ALONE IN CANADA

In 1953, Bernardus Nolte and his wife left the Netherlands to start a new life in Canada. When they arrived in Toronto, they had only $60 between them.

"In those days, you were on your own after admittance to Canada; there were no social programs. We had to find our own way for lodging etc. and finding a job. Our knowledge of English was helpful... but we had some difficulty [with Canadian accents]. We were able to rent a room for $3 a night. My wife and I found jobs the next week, although not in our field [Bernardus was a medical instrument maker]. The first two years were very hard but we survived, and we are glad that we took the big step."

11

YU HUI'S STORY: TRAGEDY IN MORECAMBE BAY

In February 2004, 21 Chinese shellfish pickers drowned in Morecambe Bay in Lancashire, England. Most of them had entered Britain illegally and were working to pay off their smuggling debts. They died because their employers made them go out onto the bay at a time when it was dangerous to do so—the pickers were trapped by rising tides. One of the migrants, Yu Hui, had phoned his family in China not long before his death, telling them about his life abroad.

"The work is very hard, and I don't even know when and how much I'll get paid. I want to quit, but I have no freedom, no choice, because I'm illegal."

Shellfish pickers set out to work across the sands of Morecambe Bay.

Illegal migration

Migrants from non-developed countries cannot legally go to live in a developed country unless they have applied to be with a close family member or they are able to arrange a job before they travel. Many therefore travel illegally. This usually means paying smugglers a lot of money to produce false identity and travel documents and arrange the journey. Smugglers can demand thousands of dollars for these services. Some people borrow money to pay for them.

Paying off debts

These migrants arrive in their destination country in debt; they have to pay the money back by working. It can take years to pay back smuggling debts. Not all migrants who arrive illegally can achieve legal status once they arrive, and many risk working illegally in the country. They lead very insecure lives, often moving from one place to another to prevent the authorities from detecting them. They may also take physical risks in the type of work they do in order to keep their jobs.

Competition

Once migrants have paid off smuggling debts, many try to save money to support their families back home. Because many migrants travel on their own, they tend to view their time in the new country as temporary and put up with long working hours and harsh living conditions to make as much money as they can. Some will work for lower wages than others, and this can cause competition among migrant worker communities.

Two housekeepers change the sheets in a hotel bedroom. Many hotels struggle to find enough local people to fill all their jobs.

AS A MATTER OF FACT

Some people accuse migrants and immigrants of taking away jobs from local people and taking advantage of state-provided services, such as healthcare and education. In fact, most migrants and immigrants of working age pay more in taxes than citizens of their new countries and use fewer services. Sometimes foreign workers may compete with locals for manual or low-skilled jobs in industries such as catering or manufacturing, but they will take those jobs that local people often avoid because of poor wages and anti-social hours.

Working anywhere

Traditionally, immigrants have settled in cities, where there are more job opportunities and more people from their home countries. But this trend is changing. As more people work abroad for shorter periods of time—to earn money rather than settle down—it is the availability of work that decides where they will go. Today, many migrants work on large farms or factories set up in industrial zones outside cities or in the countryside. These migrants often move from one place to another to keep earning money.

Driving a rickshaw in New York provides temporary employment for some immigrants.

BERNABE'S STORY: AWAY FROM HOME AND FAMILY

Mexican migrant Bernabe Garay spent 20 years moving from one place to another in the U.S., picking fruit and vegetables. He wrote this letter—one of many he sent to his family back home—from Phoenix, Arizona.

"I write this letter to greet you, hoping that when you hold this letter in your hands you will be enjoying perfect health, as mine is, thanks be to God. About renewing the contract, I can tell you nothing right now, because the boss has not told us anything yet. But I believe he will renew [it]…. He is very kind to us: there are only two of us, and he gives us watermelons, small bags with peaches, a half-dozen eggs. God willing, we will stay here with him."

Accommodation

While migrant workers are able to make more money abroad than in their home country, they usually earn less than local workers and cannot afford decent accommodations. Very often, migrant workers stay in accommodations controlled by their employers, who either provide it directly or through landlords who rent out rooms to workers. These accommodations are often of a poor standard and may be overcrowded, with several people sharing one room.

This mother and her two daughters live in one tiny room.

Workers' rights

Many migrant workers do not know their rights as workers, or the responsibilities their employers have toward them. If they work illegally, they have no immigration status and therefore no rights. There is a big risk that employers will exploit them—for example, by not paying them on time or firing them without any reason. While legal migrants and immigrants do have rights, they may fear that if they stand up for such rights they will lose their jobs.

YURIY'S STORY: EXPLOITATION IN PORTUGAL

Yuriy, who is 40 years old and from the Ukraine, found illegal work with a circus in Portugal. He describes his poor accommodations and working conditions:

"I had to sleep on the floor in a place full of fleas and rats. I had no bathroom, and I had to work 14 hours per day. Because we didn't have security in the place that we were sleeping, we gave all our documents to our boss. At the end I was so tired...that I decided to leave. I asked for my documents and my salary, but the [boss] just threw stones at me and I had to run away."

Barriers to work

One group of new arrivals in foreign countries is usually banned from working. These are asylum seekers—people who have left their home country because of persecution and who ask another country to accept them as refugees. Governments ban them from working because they hope it will keep other people from applying for asylum if they cannot legally get into a country by any other means. Because they are not usually allowed to work, asylum seekers have to rely on basic government handouts or on help from people they know.

ABED'S STORY: A DESTITUTE ASYLUM SEEKER

Abed is 19 and from northern Iraq. He was persecuted because he is a Kurd, and he fled to western Europe but was left without help or support while waiting for a decision on his case. He was also not allowed to work.

"Yesterday I slept at the mosque, and the day before in a church. I slept 11 days rough—believe me, I couldn't sleep for 5 minutes. I was so scared I walked around. I look for food in garbage cans. I find chips, for example. I eat once a day and get food at the church. I have been wearing the same jeans for two weeks, and I don't have money for transport. I feel bad about the asylum system and my current situation, and I have a lot of questions. What have I done wrong?"

Living in limbo

Many asylum seekers flee persecution because of their involvement in the politics of their home country—they might be politicians themselves, or teachers, journalists, or lawyers. These people obviously have skills and work experience, but they are unable to use them. Waiting for a decision on an asylum application can take anywhere from a few weeks to several months, and asylum seekers have to live in uncertainty during this time.

Integration

Some asylum seekers spend time improving their language skills and may also decide to do voluntary work in order to make friends and be useful to their communities. But this is not always easy, particularly if the government places asylum seekers in rural areas where they may encounter local hostility. Many asylum seekers remain unable to take part in community life and, if they are allowed to stay in their new country, find it very difficult to settle down. However, given the opportunity, others achieve great success.

ADUEI'S STORY: TAKING THE OPPORTUNITY

Aduei's family fled the war in Sudan in 1987, but she got separated from her family when rebels attacked their refugee camp in Ethiopia. She fled with others to Kenya and was allowed to resettle in the U.S. Aduei speaks five languages and is now preparing for college entrance exams. She works after school at a local pharmacy.

"Like Dr. Martin Luther King, Jr., I have a dream. I want to do something with people like me. When I look back and see young girls like me in Sudan, it bothers me."

Aduei's dream is to set up a Sudanese girls' school. If this doesn't work, she wants to try to give at least two or three girls a chance at a better life through scholarships.

Evening language classes enable immigrants to learn outside their working hours.

17

Workers line up for the bus at rush hour. Some may face discrimination at work when they get there.

Documentation

If we want to work in another country, we have to have documents—called work visas or permits—showing that we are allowed to work there. Employers are normally required to check whether someone is allowed to work before hiring him or her. In some countries, employers can face heavy fines if they employ someone who is not allowed to work. But employers are not immigration officers and may know little about immigration law. It can be difficult for them to know if an immigrant or migrant can work.

Difficulties getting work

Some employers are so afraid of being fined by the authorities for hiring undocumented workers that they might not want to hire any foreign-looking people at all. This view inevitably affects immigrants and migrants, who can face an unfair disadvantage when trying to get a job.

18

AS A MATTER OF FACT

Discrimination is the act of treating people or groups differently from other people or groups—often based on the color of their skin or their background. Employers can discriminate against foreign workers in lots of ways. One way is if an employer only asks some, and not all, new employees to prove they are entitled to work. Another way is to give a job to an immigrant with permanent legal status instead of an asylum seeker with a temporary work permit when both people are equally qualified for that job.

Difficulties at work

Immigrants need to know exactly what documents they must have to prove they can work—and so avoid losing out on a job. But discrimination can also happen once immigrants, and all people from ethnic minorities, are in a job. They may face prejudice from their colleagues or discrimination in terms of benefits or promotion. Developed countries therefore have antidiscrimination laws to ensure that people can go to court to challenge any discrimination they suffer because of their origin.

Young people consider some job options at a German job center. Finding one's first job is rarely easy.

AN ENTREPRENEUR'S STORY: FINDING A CAREER

A man from Pakistan emigrated to Denmark at the age of 15 to join his parents, who were working there. In 1990, he graduated as an engineer and started searching for work, which turned out to be very difficult—he believed it was as a result of racial prejudice. He enrolled in graduate school evening classes to upgrade his qualifications and increase his chances of getting work. After being unemployed for some time, despite applying for everything possible, he was sent to do job training in a recycling center. With no work after five years, he decided to start his own business selling watercolor paper, which later turned to handmade letter paper and envelopes.

19

Immigrant communities

Abdul is a 22-year-old who fled the troubled Ivory Coast in West Africa. He initially went to neighboring Burkina Faso before he managed to get a flight to France and arrive in Britain via the Channel Tunnel train service. He applied for asylum at Waterloo station in London. When he arrived, he spoke only French, and he had no money or possessions.

"Life was very bad when I came to Britain. When I arrived, I knew no one: I had to confront all the problems alone. No friends, no work, no anything. Every day now I am sad. I think I'm beginning to have mental problems, stress. The solution is to let me do something, go to school, learn something. How I live here is hard. I hope for the future. I pray for this."

How well immigrants integrate into life in a new country can depend on the immediate circumstances they find on arrival. For example, many immigrant women joining their husbands in a new country do not speak its language and may only have contact with relatives or friends from their own community. Refugees are often particularly disorientated, as they are still coming to terms with the trauma of war or the persecution they have suffered back home.

Community support

Over many years of immigration, communities of fellow nationals develop in different countries and cities. These communities can be a valuable source of help and contacts for new arrivals—often providing the only source of information they feel they can trust. Communities can have different meeting points and centers, such as places of religious worship, cafés and bars, and more formal associations, such as the Bangladesh-American Center in Houston, Texas, for Bangladeshi immigrants.

A meeting at the Bangladesh-American Center in Houston, Texas.

China Town, Sydney, Australia. Chinese communities across the world assist new arrivals.

LIN LIJIAN'S STORY: PAYING FOR WORK

For new arrivals, fellow nationals' help sometimes comes at a price. Lin Lijian came from China to Europe. He had no contacts when he arrived, so he paid money to a Chinese recruitment agency. He was then promptly offered a job in a Chinese restaurant as a kitchen assistant. Some people think this is exploitation; others argue that it is just how a different culture works. Lin Lijian, like most Chinese immigrants, did not see an issue in paying a Chinese acquaintance money for providing a job on his arrival. If necessary, he would have also paid someone to find him lodging.

Being independent

Some newcomers may deliberately avoid contact with their fellow nationals. Educated immigrants who can speak the language of their new country are often less inclined to seek help or support from members of their own community. This may be simply because they have less need: they can get a job more easily or might have one waiting for them on their arrival. It can also be because they want to integrate into their new society immediately.

21

Gathering information

For many immigrants, being in touch with people from their own community is not just useful when they first arrive in a new country. Community groups or contacts can continue to help immigrants stay informed about events in their own country. Where communities have settled in a certain area, there are often shops selling imported newspapers and cafés with access to TV channels from home. These places also allow immigrants to catch up on gossip.

Refugee communities

For refugees who have fled government persecution at home, contact with members of their own community can prompt them to become politically active abroad. Many people from Colombia, for example, continue to fight for human rights in their home country while living abroad. Before the fall of Iraq's Saddam Hussein in 2003, Iraqi refugees around the world demonstrated against his regime.

EDRIS'S STORY: IRAQI REFUGEE

Edris fled Iraq and went to Britain, where he was granted refugee status in 1993. In 1996, he talked about his political activities in exile:

"In Britain, I am a representative of my organization in the Iraqi Democratic Alliance, and we carry out political activities, give some lectures, and do some publishing. We are holding a continuous picket in Trafalgar Square [in London], asking that Saddam Hussein is put before an international tribunal. When I came here, I engaged too much in political activities in my first and second year.... Of course, I am looking to go back, and we have to prepare."

Faith communities

For many immigrant groups, religion plays an important role in community and family life. Jewish communities in cities around the world build synagogues to worship in, while people originally from Arab and Asian countries build mosques or Hindu or Sikh temples. These religious places act as useful meeting points for community members. They also enable families to pass knowledge on to children about their culture and religion. Without these links, it can be difficult to practice one's religion.

MAZIAH'S STORY:
ADAPTING TO A NEW CULTURE

Maziah, a Muslim from Saudi Arabia, is a graduate student in the U.S., where she has lived for the past eight years. She has three sons, ages 13, 14, and 17. She is concerned that they receive no religious education outside of the home. She thinks that when they go back to their country, her children may have problems:

"It's hard because I am in the home and teach them [about religion], and when they go outside there is nobody else that does the same thing, like praying five times a day...and I keep talking to them to do it but it is very difficult. In Saudi Arabia, it comes time to pray and everybody goes to the mosque and they go with their friends, but here I have to keep reminding them why it is important to pray."

A mosque in a new housing development in Amsterdam caters to some of the Netherlands' Muslim community.

Immigrant areas

Wherever immigrants go, they tend to settle in areas where other immigrants from their own country have already settled. In major cities such as New York, London, or Sydney, different immigrant groups live and run businesses in particular districts.

Following the crowds

Immigration today follows similar patterns to immigration in the past. For example, in the 19th- and early 20th-century U.S., many immigrants came from Europe to work in the rapidly expanding manufacturing industries. Large numbers settled near the ports where they first arrived in cities such as New York, Boston, Pittsburgh, and Chicago. They often lived in very poor conditions but were attracted by the low rent, the possibility of work, and some community support.

Many immigrants lived in crowded conditions such as this in early 20th-century New York.

Brixton in South London has become famous for its well-established African-Caribbean community.

Moving away

It was perhaps not surprising that many immigrants who lived in these poor conditions wanted to move out as soon as their earnings allowed so they would not be looked down upon by other sections of society. Their place was taken by new arrivals to the country, possibly from a different part of the world, so the community makeup would change. In New York, the Irish community of the 19th century gave way to the Italian and Jewish communities in the 20th century. Similarly, in Britain, Bangladeshi immigrants settled around Brick Lane in East London in the mid-20th century and occupied what had once been a strongly Jewish area.

Breaking patterns

There are always exceptions to these patterns. Where immigrants speak the host country's language and pursue job opportunities outside of their particular ethnic area, they are more likely to move to non-immigrant parts of a city or outside the city altogether. The patterns change, too, with the availability of work and the need for a workforce. Today, the majority of immigrants to the U.S. are from Mexico and Central America. Many concentrate in cities close to the U.S.-Mexican border, such as San Antonio in Texas or Phoenix in Arizona, to find jobs in the many companies that have set up there.

Settling in

Leaving friends and relatives behind is hard for anyone, but for children and young people, making a new start in a new school can be particularly hard. First, they will not know any other children. Second, if the school has few children from different ethnic backgrounds, they may find it difficult to make friends quickly because the other children may be suspicious of them or even have prejudices against them.

Schoolgirls discuss their work. School is one of many challenges facing immigrant children.

NAMRATA'S STORY: A DIFFICULT START

Namrata Nayar was born in India but came to the U.S. with her family to live with her aunt in North Carolina when she was 15. After arriving, Namrata attended special English language classes for foreign students.

"I found it very difficult when I came to the U.S. because I couldn't understand anyone. It was tough. I didn't understand a word anyone said, and I used to cry out in frustration. But, in the end, it didn't take that long, and I learned English fairly quickly."

Namrata went to college two years later and obtained a degree in electrical engineering. She now works for a computer software company in Raleigh, North Carolina.

A young immigrant woman interprets for her mother.

YANIRA'S STORY: HELPING HER MOTHER

When Yanira emigrated with her family from El Salvador to California, she quickly picked up English at school. However, she was often asked to translate for her mother, who could only speak Spanish. She found doing this "embarrassing." But her mother, who is uneducated, has actively encouraged Yanira to "be something, like a lawyer." Yanira, 13 years old, wants to become a meteorologist.

Standing out

Many immigrant children arrive in a new country not knowing the language and may have had little schooling back in their home country. These factors can make it hard for children to learn and progress unless they get extra support from teachers. Refugee children can face the additional problem of name-calling, because other children may view them as poor or may have heard negative stories about refugees in the media.

Extra efforts

Despite—or perhaps because of—the hard time they can face, many immigrant and refugee children are very ambitious. They often do well at school against all the odds. But immigrant children often have to work hard at home, too. Because children usually pick up new languages more quickly than adults, parents may use them as interpreters whenever they need to deal with the authorities.

27

Different experiences

Despite the challenges posed by school, young people tend to have a more positive experience than older people of adjusting to life in a new country. One reason is that the expectations of parents and grandparents can be quite different from those of their children—particularly if they did not want to leave their country but were forced to flee because of war or persecution. They may be reluctant or find it too hard to adjust to life in a strange country, and maintain hopes of returning home against all odds.

TINA'S STORY: ADAPTING TO A NEW LIFE

Tina Duong's family fled Vietnam in 1975. Her brother sponsored her to go and live in the U.S.

"When we first arrived, we had trouble because we didn't speak English very well. We weren't accustomed to the...way of life in the U.S. I couldn't use the oven, turn on the shower, or vacuum the floor because I hadn't encountered these things in my homeland. Eventually, I overcame the tough times and got to learn how things work with hard work and determination. We now have a very happy family, a nice house, and a successful business. My children are studying hard in school and are bound to be successful in the future."

Holding on

If migrants hope to return home, they will make less effort to integrate into their new society because they regard their time abroad as temporary. They may only keep in touch with relatives or other fellow nationals and live according to their own customs and values. Others, however, will continue to respect their own culture while adopting some aspects of the new society in which they live.

These African refugee children wear the clothes of their new country, while their mothers remain in the clothes of their own culture.

```
        #809  01-27-2019 4:41PM
    Item(s) checked out to p1732170.

TITLE: The bad beginning
BC: 32091026165929
DUE: 02-17-19

TITLE: The tiger rising
BC: 32091029365609
DUE: 02-17-19

TITLE: One country to another
BC: 32091036568641
DUE: 02-17-19

TITLE: Bound for America : the story of
BC: 32091029180669
DUE: 02-17-19

TITLE: Life as an immigrant
BC: 32091036212984
DUE: 02-17-19

TITLE: Immigrants
BC: 3 2091 01867 5505
DUE: 02-17-19


    Support the Library you love.
  Join The Friends. www.thefriends.org
```

This Tamil girl is adapting well to her new life in Europe.

Culture clash

Many immigrant parents feel it is important to pass on the native customs and language of their home country to their children. Many feel disappointed if their children adopt a different lifestyle. But this different lifestyle is inevitable for many young people who find it increasingly difficult to see their future back in their parents' country. This can sometimes lead to immigrant children trying to discard their own nationality and cultural identity completely, causing conflict with their parents.

THILEPAN'S STORY: CHANGING WORLDS

Thilepan and his wife left Sri Lanka 19 years ago to settle in Naples, Italy. Their two children were born in Italy.

"I passed my first five years as an illegal immigrant with a lot of difficulties, and then fortunately I got my work permit.... But it is very, very difficult for me to forget about my past. I am living here with my wife and my two sons [nine and five]. I come from a completely different mentality, culture, religion, costume, way of living.... Like it or not, I am obligated to accept certain things of this Italian society.... The real difficulty I am finding now is growing and integrating my children into this society. It is not so easy a duty. I must help them to not forget about their roots, their origin, their language, and their story. But in this society, I and my family, like many other immigrants, have got a lot of problems only for our skin color. So what will happen for our children in the future?"

29

Experiencing racism

Racism can affect all ethnic minority groups, but immigrants are often particular targets. Research shows that most immigrants in the developed world have suffered from some form of racism, whether hostility, harassment, or even violence. Today, increasing numbers of asylum seekers apply to stay in European countries such as Britain, Germany, France, and Italy. While the authorities process their applications, they house many of them in areas with a mainly white local population. Easily identifiable as foreigners, the asylum seekers are often subjected to racial abuse.

AYMAN'S STORY: FROM RWANDA TO RACISM

In the early 1990s, Ayman fled the genocide in Rwanda. He applied for asylum in Germany and was sent to a refugee hostel in a small, isolated village in eastern Germany.

"There were rumors that skinheads were active in this part of eastern Germany. I was filled with dread and anxiety. I arrived in Zemmin on November 23, 1994. The next day...I was attacked by two skinheads. Later, when I was making a telephone call from a public phone booth, I was verbally abused by a group of young men who followed me all the way back to the hostel and informed the director that blacks were not welcome. As far as I am aware, the director took no action with the police."

Asylum seekers died in this arson attack on a hostel in Germany.

New arrivals line up to register for asylum at an immigration office.

Being different

As racism tends to be mainly directed at people who are of non-white appearance, immigrants from Asia, Africa, and Latin America are usually more exposed to it than immigrants from, for example, eastern Europe or Russia. But racism is not just a modern phenomenon. When Asians, notably Chinese, first arrived in California in the 19th century, they encountered hostility from the local population because they looked different and had very different habits and customs.

Economic reasons

Today, travel, television, and the Internet mean that fear of strangers is a less common reason for people to display racist behavior toward foreigners. Instead, many people think that immigrants take away their jobs and drain their country's economy. They see foreigners as a threat to their own security and national identity. The news media occasionally encourages such fears by running negative stories about immigration. Politicians can also encourage these views by arguing that governments need to be tougher on immigration—they know this argument can win them votes with the local population.

WARSAN'S STORY: REFUGEE TREATMENT

Warsan's family fled the civil war in Somalia in 1991 and spent two years in Kenya before going to Europe. Warsan feels very bitter about how governments in developed countries treat refugees.

"The term 'asylum seeker' is problematic. 'Asylum' has the connotation of a mental institution. It's implying that we're crazy, dangerous people. I have no problem with the term 'refugee,' as it is accurate—we are seeking refuge, sanctuary. If Somalia had peace, we wouldn't be here in our tens of thousands. Everywhere in Somalia, a weapon made in Europe or America is haunting me. They don't let us live in peace, and we're persecuted here as well."

31

Gaining citizenship

Once immigrants have been in a country for a number of years, many inevitably think about whether to adopt the nationality of that country. For the majority of immigrants, the motivation is often less about completely identifying with the culture and society of their new home, and more about practical issues. Gaining citizenship of a developed country, for example, means that they can vote or stand in elections and travel abroad with fewer restrictions.

ROSE'S STORY:
HELPING THE CHILDREN

Rose Kaye left Germany to work in Britain in the 1950s. She got married and had two children, and then decided to acquire British citizenship.

"The main reason for me to become British was that I thought that if things did not work out with my husband, then I would not be tempted to go back to Germany and uproot the children from school and their friends and relatives in Britain. Becoming British meant I made a commitment to stay."

Rose and her husband stayed happily married, however, and their children still live and work in Britain. She keeps in regular contact with her family in Germany.

Rose with her husband Harold.

32

Becoming a new citizen

What nationality people hold usually depends on the nationality of their parents and which country they themselves were born in. For immigrants building a new life in another country, applying for citizenship of that country may mean giving up their old nationality. Usually, they have to prove that they have legally lived in the country for a number of years, can speak the language, and have already made a new life for themselves.

A new identity

Adapting to life in a new country does not always involve thinking too much about one's national identity. Many people today, including immigrants, have begun to question the meaning of national identity. Some may feel that it doesn't really matter what national identity they have. For these people, identifying with the things they do in daily life is more important.

ZAFIR'S STORY: THE MEANING OF BELONGING

Zafir Behlic became a refugee when he fled the war in Bosnia in the early 1990s. Having made a life for himself far from his home country, he describes his feelings about his identity.

"I am like millions of migrants and refugees across the world who, despite working extremely hard to become British, Australian, or North American and putting even more effort into staying Bosnian, Vietnamese, or Irish, end up being neither of the two. Yet, every day, I feel more settled, more fulfilled, more 'integrated,' if you like. It is not the nationality or politics or the geography of a place that defines me. What defines me is what I do every day, the people I love, what I achieve, what I believe in, and the languages I speak. That's where the sense of belonging comes from for me."

Making a mark

Governments in the developed world are gradually acknowledging the contributions that immigrants have made to their respective countries, culturally and, especially, economically. The railroads in the U.S. would not have been built without the work of many immigrants in the 19th century. Today, farming in developed countries largely depends on the work of migrants.

MADRIGAL'S STORY: WORKING HARD FOR A SEASON

Madrigal is a 24-year-old from Mexico who has been sent to North Carolina to work on a large farm. This is what a typical working day is like for Madrigal:

"At six, the supervisors show up to transport the workers to the fields. Today's task is digging sweet potatoes, and I will spend the next 10 hours on my knees, knife in hand, cutting off the roots and filling a red pail with tubers. I make 35 cents for every pail I empty onto the grower's truck, which means I must fill and dump at least 20 pails an hour if I want to earn more than my base wage of $6.98. I work so fast that I keep gouging myself with the knife."

Individual achievement

Immigrants' financial contributions to national economies are significant. This achievement becomes even more remarkable given the hardship some immigrants face when trying to build a new life. Often, they arrive on their own, leaving their families behind, with no guarantees that they will be able to secure a steady job and a stable income for their family's future. Many have no knowledge of the language and barely speak it even after years in the country.

Immigrant workers on an industrial farm in the U.S.

Professional work

For immigrants with professional qualifications, eventual success comes at a price. Many take up work in low-skilled jobs when they first arrive, in the hope of being able to practice their profession in the future. Some may have to retrain before their professional qualifications will be recognized in their new country— it can take years before they save enough money to afford this. Even when they can practice again, having not worked in their profession for years, it takes time to develop confidence once more.

LIGIA'S STORY: FROM DENTIST TO CLEANER

Ligia qualified as a dentist in Romania in the 1950s but decided to go to Germany, where there were better career prospects. But she spent almost nine years working as a cleaner. She then married and eventually took up German citizenship, and was able to start the long process of requalifying to practice as a dentist.

"I didn't want to leave, and I came to Germany to work. Just to work. I didn't mind what work I was doing as long as I could work and at least earn some money. I run my own dental practice now, but it took a long time and a lot of money. I spent years working as an assistant in other dental practices so I could eventually pass the exams."

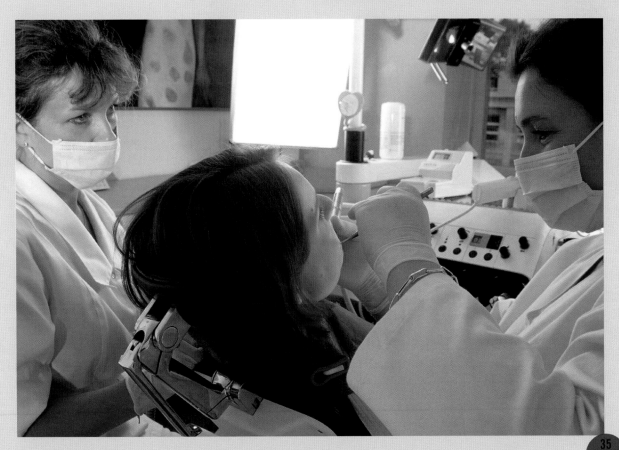

A dentist at work. Immigrants with professional experience in occupations such as dentistry must often retrain and start their familiar profession from the bottom and work their way back up.

Changing plans

Many immigrants and migrants start out with the plan of earning money for their families back home and then returning to join them. These plans can change, however. Over time, some immigrants start saving in the host country and improve their lifestyle. For many, this is an incentive to stay abroad much longer than they had originally planned. For those who do not return home, it may mean they lose touch with their family. If they leave their wife or husband behind, it may mean separation and a new family life for both partners.

New buildings in southern China. Many of these have been built with money sent home by immigrants.

Earning power

Many immigrants and migrants send substantial amounts of their earnings back home. Often, the poorer the family back home, the more money a person will send, because it can be vital for survival. This puts a lot of pressure on immigrants to earn as much as possible. But if immigrants earn more than they expected

MENG DONG'S STORY: SEEKING SUCCESS

In 1999, Meng Dong's parents paid $50,000 for a smuggler to take him from China to the U.S. He was 15. His parents had heard success stories from other families who had sent their children abroad. Meng Dong changed his name to Jack and initially found work in a family friend's restaurant but found it difficult moving beyond this. Although Jack now has permission to stay in the U.S. and is settled, he dissuades others from making the same journey.

"[Young immigrants] never tell people in China they are having a difficult time, only how good they are doing here. They say they are getting fat even though they are bone. People's life in China is based on socialization. They ask, 'How is your son doing?' And they say, 'Oh my son is doing so great.' And that encourages everybody to come to the United States. Some guys think they are fat or ugly, but if they come here and make money, they can marry someone beautiful. Don't come, just focus on whatever your current education is. There's always ways to have a better future."

Meng Dong's story featured in the New York newspaper *Downtown Express* in February 2004.

to abroad, they tend to send less of their earnings back home. This is because they feel less secure about investing their money in their home country, and also because the more money they earn in their host country, the more they spend there.

Choices

The ability to start saving and building an independent life abroad opens up new options for immigrants. They may think about investing money in their home country at some point in the future—if the political and financial situation is stable. On the other hand, they may plan for a long-term future in the host country and may be able to help other family members come to join them abroad.

AS A MATTER OF FACT

When migrants or immigrants decide to return to their home country, they bring with them not only money they may have saved. Any skills that they have gained abroad, such as a language or professional training, can benefit their country. A controversial form of migration in recent years has been the number of doctors from African countries who go to work in Europe and the U.S. Some people argue that this migration drains poorer countries of vitally needed medical staff. Others point out that many of these doctors do go back, and they have learned new techniques and procedures during their time away.

An African doctor at work in a Norwegian hospital. Many developed countries need immigrant nurses and doctors to keep their health services running.

Thinking of the future

The thought of returning to one's home country is never far away for some immigrants. It may even occur to their children or grandchildren, especially if the political or economic situation in the home country improves. In the 1990s, Ireland's economy flourished. Many Americans of Irish origin therefore returned to Ireland to take advantage of new work opportunities.

Helping rebuild

For some, the question of returning home has particular significance. Refugees who have fled their country because of war or persecution often continue to feel very connected to their homeland. They hope to return sooner rather than later—provided the situation has improved. Younger refugees are more likely to want to stay in their new country so that they can at least gain skills or qualifications, which they can use in their native country when they do decide to go back.

KUEI AND YAI'S STORY: LONGING FOR HOME

Kuei is a Sudanese refugee who arrived in Australia with her sister and five children in September 2002. Her husband Yai Dut Atem originally fled to the U.S. from Sudan. He married Kuei during a short visit in 2003 but has to return regularly to the U.S. until he is granted permanent residence status in Australia.

"Our main hope for the future is for the best education possible for our family, and a good life for our son, Atem. We want to be able to return to Sudan one day, when there is peace, and help to educate the poor, and teach them in every way we can."

38

Bomb damage in Baghdad, 2005. It is still difficult for Iraqi refugees to return there.

NAZAR'S STORY: GOING HOME

Nazar is a refugee from Iraq. After more than 20 years of not having been back to his country, he finally went to visit his family in Baghdad in 2003.

"The day I arrived in Baghdad was like a dream come true. It was very hot, and there was a lot of traffic in the streets. But I also felt like I was in a completely different city. Nothing looked like I remembered it. I even struggled to recognize my family's house. [My family] all ran toward me—what an emotional time for us all! Of course, to bridge the gap after 20 years is not easy. It will take many visits just to keep the contact with my family and my home country."

Visiting home

Governments in host countries sometimes try to encourage refugees and other immigrants from certain countries to visit their home country to see if conditions are right for them and their families to return. For example, the British government has set up a special program for immigrants and refugees from Afghanistan to give them the opportunity to visit their country to see if they want to return there permanently. This can put pressure on their communities and also divide families, especially when the younger generation does not want to return to their home country at all.

A refugee gets advice about his options for returning home.

39

Schools can help to make immigrant children start to feel at home.

A new home

Other immigrants may have few, if any, thoughts of returning home. This is often because their families have firmly established themselves in the new country. They may in fact not have many relatives left in their home country—and so have little to return to. In addition, many immigrant families have children born in the host country. The ability of children to quickly integrate into their new society can help parents feel more at home.

Different experiences

Migrants' experiences can be very different to those of immigrants. Migrants are more likely to return to their home country once they have saved enough money to improve their family's quality of life. Often they have no choice: most are not allowed to settle in the destination country for

good. In contrast, immigrants who are allowed to stay are in a better position to secure their financial situation. With a better lifestyle abroad, it is hard for them to consider returning home.

An uncertain future

For anyone going to live and work abroad, the first few years will certainly be challenging and full of uncertainties. It usually takes a long time before an immigrant is able to get permission to settle permanently, and, without this guarantee, many find life difficult because they are never sure if they will be able stay. This situation is unlikely to improve. Governments will probably restrict immigration laws even further in the future, and this could affect migrants' and immigrants' ability to apply for permanent residence.

Many immigrant families start out their new lives in America in small towns.

MARK'S STORY: ONCE RUSSIAN, NOW AMERICAN

Mark Sashine and his wife, son, and mother-in-law are a Russian-Jewish family. They left Russia via Austria and now live in the U.S. Here, Mark describes his family's new life:

"We went through the interview process in Europe and were lucky to be admitted. I got my first job at a small engineering company with a lot of immigrants in it. The owner was a mechanical buff and somewhat of an environmentalist. That was another piece of luck for us. There was no problem with my accent because it was only one of many. Thanks to that job, my wife could enroll in the university English courses, and we settled as real Americans in a small town of about 5,000 residents. Our son went out to the street...and returned from it not a Russian anymore. Of us four, our son is the first person who talks English and Spanish much better than Russian, and we speak English with him. We both, of course, are fluent in English. Our granny still speaks Russian only.

Due to the job I got, we skipped the usual process of assimilation within the community of the people of the same kind, like in New York, Boston, or any other place where there are big Russian-Jewish settlements. We liked the idea and decided for ourselves that whenever possible we will be on our own, belong to no group, and cherish our independence. We've kept this resolution so far, but it is not without a price. Both of us are relatively successful now. I lost my first job, had several others. We moved several times. My wife studied, then worked full-time. Now we work for a big company. I am an engineer, and my wife is a manager. Our son studies in a good university. We all are U.S. citizens."

41

Glossary

arson To set fire to a building deliberately.

asylum Special legal immigration status given to people who are recognized as refugees according to the 1951 Convention on Refugees.

asylum seeker A person seeking asylum in another country because he or she fears persecution or danger in his or her own country.

citizenship If a person has a country's citizenship, it means he or she is a national of that country and holds that country's passport.

developed countries High-income countries where people have a high standard of living. These are usually found in Europe and North America, but also include Australia, New Zealand, and Japan.

developing countries Low- and middle-income countries where people have a lower standard of living and not as many goods and services available to them as in developed countries.

discrimination Treating people differently, and usually unfairly, because of their age, sex, nationality, color, or because of a disability.

emigrate To leave one's home country to live permanently in another country.

entrepreneur A person setting up a business.

ethnic Belonging or relating to a cultural or racial group.

exile Living outside one's home country against one's will.

exploitation In a workplace situation, treating employees in a way that suits the interests of the business without respecting the interests of the individual.

genocide The mass murder of a particular race or ethnic group of people.

Hindu A follower of Hinduism, a religion whose history dates back more than 5,000 years. Today it is mostly practiced in India.

immigrant A person who has moved permanently to another country to live and work.

immigration laws Laws that set out the circumstances under which people can live and work in a country not their own.

industrial zone An area of land earmarked for businesses and factories only.

Jew A follower of the religion of Judaism, a religion originating in the Middle East and dating back more than 4,000 years. A Jew may also be an ethnic description of a person who traces his or her roots back to the Hebrews, the people who founded Judaism.

migrant A person going to work in another country, usually for a limited time only.

mosque A Muslim place of worship.

Muslim A follower of Islam, a religion founded by the Prophet Muhammad in Saudi Arabia in the seventh century A.D.

national A person who belongs to a particular nation or state.

persecution Being punished, tortured, or mistreated by a government or a military group, usually because of one's political or religious beliefs or ethnic backround.

racism Judging people or behaving unfairly to them because of their skin color or ethnic background.

refugee camp A settlement, usually temporary, that develops when people flee their homes during times of war or famine to go to a safer area near the borders of their own country.

refugees People living abroad who are recognized under international law as being unable to return to their home country for fear of their lives or freedom.

rights Claims to freedom, equal treatment, and resources that are guaranteed by law.

Sikh A person following Sikhism, a religion founded more than 500 years ago by the Guru Nanak in the Punjab region of the Indian subcontinent.

smuggler A person helping another person to travel illegally into another country.

synagogue A Jewish place of worship.

visa Official permission from a foreign country to visit it. This is usually given by the country's embassy, which puts a stamp in a person's passport to show that a visa has been granted.

work permit Permission given by immigration authorities in the form of a letter or a stamp in the passport to show that the person is allowed to work in the country.

Web connections

International organizations
International Organization for Migration (IOM)
www.iom.int

International Labor Organization (ILO)
www.ilo.org

United Nations (UN)
www.un.org

United Nations High Commissioner for Refugees (UNHCR)
www.unhcr.ch

Nongovernmental organizations
New York's Lower East Side Tenement Museum
The Immigrant Experience
www.tenement.org/immigrantexperience

Australian Refugee Council
www.refugeecouncil.org.au
Supports asylum seekers and refugees in Australia.

British Refugee Council
www.refugeecouncil.org.uk
Supports asylum seekers and refugees in Britain.

Electronic Immigration Network
www.ein.org.uk
On-line gateway to resources on immigration and asylum worldwide.

National Immigration Forum
www.immigrationforum.org
Works to promote the rights of immigrants and refugees in the U.S.

Pier21. National Historic Site Gateway Canada
www.pier21.ca
Site of a Canadian museum of immigration.

Government sites
Australian Department of Immigration and Multicultural and Indigenous Affairs
www.immi.gov.au

UK Home Office Immigration and Nationality Directorate
www.ind.homeoffice.gov.uk

U.S. Citizenship and Immigration Services
www.uscis.gov/graphics/index.htm

Index

accommodations 15, 24
Afghanistan 39
African-Caribbean community 25
anti-discrimination laws 19
asylum
    application for 16, 17
    seekers 16, 17, 18, 20, 30, 31
Australia 8, 21, 24, 38

Bangladeshis 20, 25
Bosnia 33
Britain 20, 22, 25, 30, 32, 39

Canada 11
Central America 25
Channel Tunnel 20
children 23, 26, 27, 40
China 12, 36
Chinese communities 21
citizenship 32, 33, 35
college 17
Colombia 22
cultural identity 29
culture 9, 23, 28, 32, 34
customs 8, 9, 28, 29

Denmark 19
developed countries 9, 12, 19, 30, 31, 32, 34
discrimination 18, 19

economy
    contributing to 34
    draining 31
education 9, 26, 27
El Salvador 27
employers 12, 15, 18
employment 18, 19
Europe 16, 21, 24, 29, 31, 37
exile 22
exploitation 15, 21

France 30

Germany 10, 19, 30, 32, 35
governments 9, 11, 16, 17, 22, 31, 34, 39, 40

healthcare 9
home country 8, 14, 33, 37, 38, 39, 40
host country 36, 37, 39, 40
hostility 9, 17, 30, 31
human rights 22

illegal immigrants 9, 12, 29
immigrant areas 24, 25
immigrant communities 5, 9, 10, 13, 21, 22, 23, 24, 25, 39
immigration laws 18, 41
India 26
integration 9, 17, 20, 21, 28, 32, 40
Iraq 16, 22, 39
Irish community 25
Italian communities 8, 25
Italians 8
Italy 29, 30
Ivory Coast 20

Jewish community 23, 25

language
    of home 29
    interpreting 27
    learning a new 17, 26, 27
    speaking 9, 21, 25, 33, 34, 41
living conditions 13, 15, 24

media 27, 31
meeting places 22, 23

Mexico 14, 25, 34
migrants 8, 10, 11, 13, 14, 18, 28, 33, 34, 36, 40
    illegal migrants 12, 15
Morecambe Bay 12
Muslims 23

nationality 29, 32, 33
nationals 8, 20, 21, 28
Netherlands 23
non-developed countries 12

Pakistan 19
persecution 10, 16, 17, 20, 22, 28, 38
politics 9, 17, 22, 31, 37, 38
Portugal 15
prejudice 9, 18, 26

racial prejudice 19
racism 31
refugees 9, 16, 20, 22, 27, 28, 30, 31, 33, 38, 39
religion 23
returning home 9, 22, 28, 36, 37, 38, 39, 40
Romania 35
Russia 31, 41
Rwanda 30

Saudi Arabia 23
school 26, 27
sending money home 36, 40
settlement patterns 14
    cities 14, 17
    industrial zones 14
    rural areas 17
skills 17, 35, 37
smuggling debts 12, 13
Somalia 31
Sri Lanka 29

state services 11, 13, 16
Sudan 17, 38

taxes 8, 13

Ukraine 15
U.S. 8, 10, 14, 17, 24, 25, 26, 27, 28, 31, 34, 36, 37, 38, 41

Vietnam 28
visa 18

war 10, 20, 28, 38
work
    availability 14
    conditions 13, 15
    dangerous 12
    documents to 16
    finding work 10, 11, 16, 17
    permit 18
    temporary 11
workers' rights 15

younger generation 9, 39